Britney Spears backstage pass

by Jan Gabriel

SCHOLASTIC INC.

New York   Toronto   London   Auckland   Sydney   Mexico City   New Delhi   Hong Kong

Photography Credits:

Front Cover: Albert Sanchez; Back Cover: Ernie Paniccioli/Retna; 3: Mark J. Terrill/AP Photo; 6, left: Todd Kaplan/Star File Photo; 6, right: David Allocca/DMI; 7, right: Todd Kaplan/Star File Photo; 8: Ernie Paniccioli/Retna; 9, lower left: Lisa Means/*People* Weekly © 1999; 9, upper right: Todd Kaplan/Star File Photo; 10, lower left: Anthony Cutajar/London Features; 10, upper right: London Features; 11 (both photos): Mark Allan/Globe Photos; 12, top left: David Allocca/DMI; 13, top left: Jen Lowery/London Features; 14: Mark Allan/Globe Photos; 15, lower right: George De Sota/London Features; 16, upper left: London Features; 17: courtesy of *16* magazine; 18, lower left and lower right: Lisa Means/*People* Weekly © 1999; 18, upper right: Mark Allan/Globe Photos; 19, bottom: Todd Kaplan/Star File Photo; 20, lower right: Lisa Means/*People* Weekly © 1999; 21, Mark Allan/Globe Photos; 22, top right: Mark Allan/Globe Photos; 22, middle; Ernie Paniccioli/Retna; 23, upper left: Jen Lowery/London Features; 23, lower right: David Allocca/DMI; 24-25: Todd Kaplan/Star File Photo; 26: Mark Allan/Globe Photos; 27, upper left: Anthony Cutajar/London Features; 27, lower left: Ernie Paniccioli/Retna; 27, lower right: Britt Carpenter/*Teen People* © 1999; 28: Todd Kaplan/Star File Photo; 29, upper right: David Allocca/DMI; 29, lower right: Mary Monaco/Shooting Star; 30, upper right: Ernie Paniccioli/Retna; 30, bottom: David Allocca/DMI; 31 (both photos): David Allocca/DMI; 32, top: David Allocca/DMI; 32, lower right: Ernie Paniccioli/Retna; 33, upper right: Jeffrey Mayer/Star File Photo; 33, bottom: Lisa Means/*People* Weekly © 1999; 34, upper right: Britt Carpenter/*Teen People* © 1999; 34, lower right: Steve Granitz/Retna; 35: Todd Kaplan/Star File Photo; 36, upper left: Mary Monaco/Shooting Star; 36, lower right: Jeffrey Mayer/Star File Photo; 37, upper right: Ernie Paniccioli/Retna; 37, bottom: David Allocca/DMI; 38, upper left: Mark Allan/Globe Photos; 39, left: Fitzroy Barrett/Globe Photos; 39, right: Larry Marano/London Features; 40: Ernie Paniccioli/Retna; 41, lower right: Ernie Paniccioli/Retna; 42: Todd Kaplan/Star File Photo; 43, lower right: Jen Lowery/London Features; 44: Mark Allan/Globe Photos; 45, lower right: Alex Lloyd Gross/Star File; 46, lower left: Steve Granitz/Retna; 46, upper right: Mary Monaco/Shooting Star; 47-48: Ernie Paniccioli/Retna.

If you purchased this book without a cover, you should be aware that this book is stolen property. It was reported as "unsold and destroyed" to the publisher, and neither the author nor the publisher has received any payment for this "stripped book."

No part of this work may be reproduced, stored in a retrieval system, or transmitted in any form or by any means, electronic, mechanical, photocopying, recording, or otherwise, without written permission of the publisher. For information regarding permission, write to Scholastic Inc., Attention: Permissions Department, 555 Broadway, New York, NY 10012.

ISBN 0-439-13548-6

Design by Peter Koblish

Copyright © 1999 Scholastic Inc. All rights reserved. Published by Scholastic Inc. SCHOLASTIC and associated logos are trademarks and/or registered trademarks of Scholastic Inc.

12   0 1 2 3 4/0

Printed in the U.S.A.
First Scholastic printing, July 1999

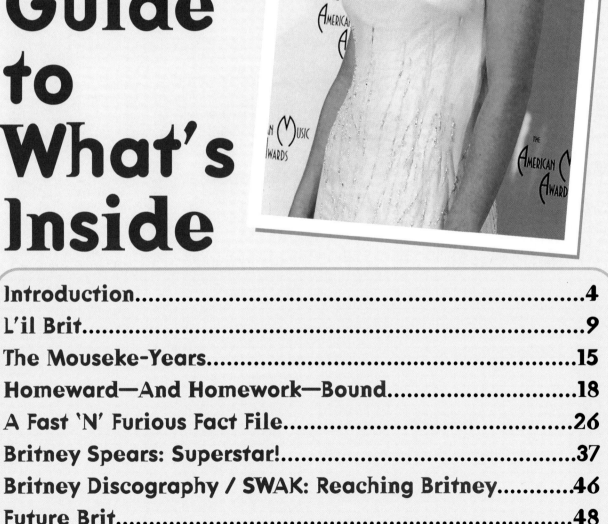

"I'm having the time of my life. All this work has paid off!"

Guide to What's Inside

Introduction
Resistance Is Futile!

Petite powerhouse Britney Spears is, quite simply, *everywhere:* on the radio, on your cassette or CD player, on MTV, on billboards, in magazines, TV shows, on the concert stage, and, suddenly, in the hearts of music-lovin' tweens and teens all over the globe. "Every girl wants to be like her, and every guy wants to get to know her." So says the president of her record company. And you know what? He's right.

This girl has got it goin' on—and on and on and on.

Having a number–one album and a number–one single at the same time made history!

That Song, That Song, That So-o-o-ng: Making Music History

Before this year, few knew her name, let alone her music. But as the calendar flipped to January 1999—it instantly became the year of Britney Spears as she blasted onto the music charts and into the music history books.

It's all, of course, due to a little ditty called "...Baby One More Time." The single, with its catchy *"Oh, bay-bay, bay-bay"* opening line was the number-one song on the *Billboard* charts—its first week out.

That was amazing in itself, until something else happened: Her very first CD did the same exact thing.

And *that* twin feat has never been accomplished before by a new female artist.

More: The single had staying power. Its chart reign continued for a cool 35 weeks, replaced only by her second song, "Sometimes."

The album also kept pace. It lodged five weeks at number one, going multi-platinum by selling over three million copies.

Cross-Country Concert-Chica

It's not just hearing her music on the radio that has captivated the country; Britney's electrifying live performances have lit up the stage. She started performing first in shopping malls; soon after, she

Britney Spears

took concert stages from Seattle to Singapore. But wherever she performs—in front of The Gap or at Carnegie Hall—whether she's headlining or opening for a group like 'N Sync, audiences go wild for her.

A Real-Life Tommy Girl

The all-out Britney attack has included a major gig as a cover girl and model for the way popular just nikki :) catalogue, where the words to "...Baby One More Time" were printed, along with a mini Q&A.

"I like the style of '...Baby One More Time,' because of the way it's written and its melody. I can add a lot of attitude."

Her song, "...Baby One More Time" hit number one in sixteen countries around the world!

Her image? As All-American as baseball, apple pie, and "Soda Pop!"

and a tank top. The fashion spread isn't limited to the glossies: Britney's on billboards all over America.

Up The Creek & Beyond

When it was announced that she signed to guest star in three episodes of the hottest teen show on TV, *Dawson's Creek,* it seemed kind of a stretch. Would she play herself? Some fictional equivalent? Not necessary: the girl is totally camera-ready. She spent two years as a Mouseketeer, singing, dancing, and acting on the Disney Channel's *The Mickey Mouse Club*. So a stint turning Dawson, Joey, Jen, and Pacey's world

Next came the even more high-profile Tommy Hilfiger modeling gig. Check out any magazine aimed at girls and young women: Britney is prominently featured in two-page advertisements, posing with headphones and Tommy jeans

upside down is totally doable.

But there's more: Britney has signed up to star—yep, you read that right—in her very own TV series, created just for her. While no details have been nailed just yet, look for a weekly dose of Brit, starting sometime next year.

Her Image:

"I kinda want to be categorized as someone who's yeah, pure...and just really sweet."

She's doing a really good job of that! Though some have carped about the lyrics of "...Baby One More Time," and others have criticized the video, the image that most people

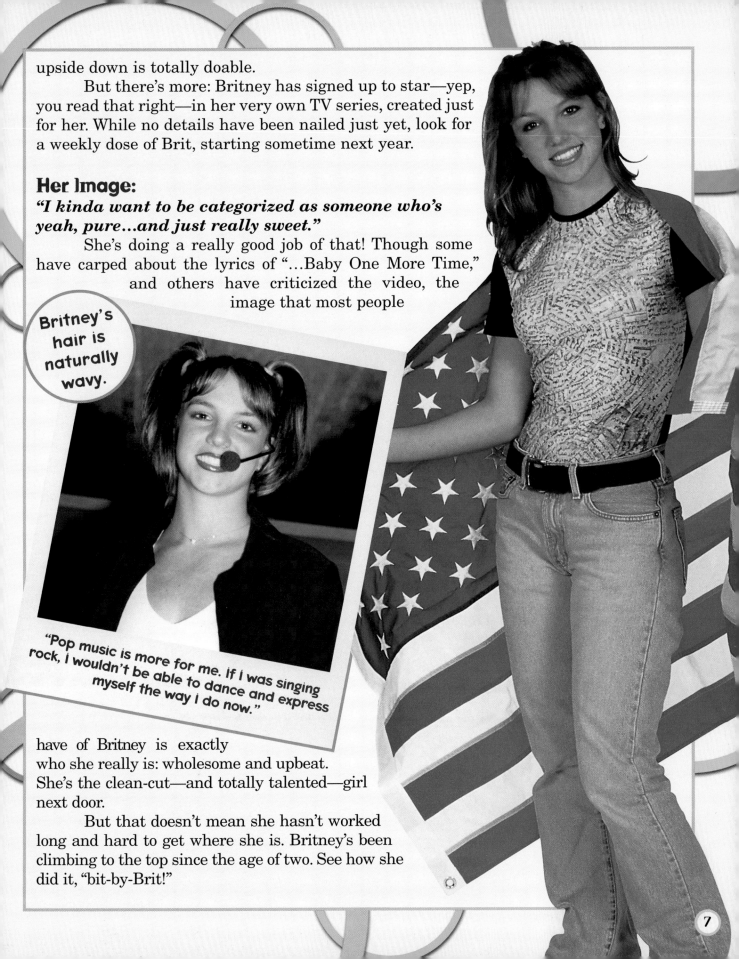

Britney's hair is naturally wavy.

"Pop music is more for me. if i was singing rock, i wouldn't be able to dance and express myself the way i do now."

have of Britney is exactly who she really is: wholesome and upbeat. She's the clean-cut—and totally talented—girl next door.

But that doesn't mean she hasn't worked long and hard to get where she is. Britney's been climbing to the top since the age of two. See how she did it, "bit-by-Brit!"

Britney Spears

L'il Brit

"I found out what I'm supposed to do at an early age."

Britney Jean was born on December 2, 1981, to Jamie and Lynne Spears, who already had a five-year-old son named Bryan. Although both her parents were professionals in their fields—he in construction, she in education—neither was particularly involved in drama, art, or music. So when little Britney, practically from the moment she could talk, started *singing*, they were surprised. Even more so when she continued—almost nonstop around the household—from the age of two on.

"I was in my own world, singing and dancing to imaginary audiences," Britney has recalled in various interviews.

Britney's a mama's girl: She bought Lynne a diamond tennis bracelet.

"This is what i've wanted to do all my life, to have an album and perform my music."

"I was always in my living room singing, I drove my mother crazy, but she got so used to it."

Her mom concurs, "She was always singing, she would never hush."

Her brother, Bryan, remembers those earliest years well. "She'd be in front of the TV, mimicking Madonna," he said, admitting that it got annoying.

As the years went on, her parents' surprise and her brother's annoyance soon turned to something else: amazement—and the realization that Britney had a special gift.

Britney told *Girls' Life* magazine, "One day I was jumping on my trampoline and singing and my mom realized I could carry a tune. I think that was when I first thought about going into entertainment."

At home, Britney roughhouses with big bro Bryan.

Hometown Girl

While the seeds of a future career may have been planted at a very young age, it would take a few years before Britney could actually do anything about it. She was, after all, just a little kid growing up in a small town called Kentwood on the Louisiana/Mississippi border. She had no showbiz connections at all.

That didn't stop her.

Britney made her "stage debut" when she was five years old. She sang "What Child Is This" at her kindergarten "graduation" ceremony. That led to more public performances. She sang in

"When people see things on TV that they can't do, that should make them want to go out there and make something of themselves. That's how I always looked at it."

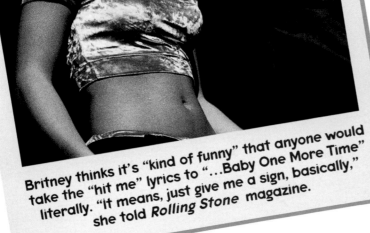

Britney thinks it's "kind of funny" that anyone would take the "hit me" lyrics to "...Baby One More Time" literally. "It means, just give me a sign, basically," she told *Rolling Stone* magazine.

the church choir, danced in local revues, and performed at any community event she could. She entered every talent show around and, at the age of six, won her first award. As she grew up, she began to book gigs at neighborhood amusement parks and local TV shows.

Her dream of being a professional entertainer grew. As her brother, Bryan, related to *People* magazine, "She would put on makeup and sing to herself in the bathroom mirror!"

Chillin' in her "girly" bedroom.

"Onstage, with all the people screaming—fast songs are simply the best."

Of course, during those tender years, Britney did everything other kids did as well: She went to school, played with her friends, took dance lessons. She also did things most other kids didn't do. "I took gymnastics lessons—even though we had to drive an hour to get there. [She went to Bela Karolyi's training camp where future Olympians train.] I live in a really small town and [that] was really unheard of. People were like, what are you doing? I'm just thankful that my mom was there to support me." In the car on the way to gymnastics, she'd sing along with the radio. Her favorite singers? Whitney Houston and Mariah Carey.

The Mickey Mouse Club: No Admittance!

When Britney was eight years old, she heard about open auditions for a TV show on the Disney Channel called *The Mickey Mouse Club*. She had to convince her parents to get on board, but eventually, with their help, she tried out. Although she impressed the casting directors, she didn't get the gig: Britney was turned away for being too young.

Not that she left the audition empty-handed. A way impressed producer of the show tipped her off to a talent agent in New York City. He suggested she go there for the summer—and get some real, professional training and advice.

Little Brit In The Big Apple

Spending the next three summers in New York City changed Britney's life—and that of her family as well. Because she was only eight, nine, and ten years old, her mom had to be with her, which meant a disruption of their family life. But by that time, it was the obvious move: Britney had precocious talent and a real hunger to share it with audiences.

"i've had to give up some stuff to do this, but i don't miss high school. When i was home two years ago, every weekend we'd go out and do the same thing. it's wonderful as long as you love what you're doing. . . . i'd rather be doing this!"

There was word that Britney would appear on TV's *Beverly Hills, 90210*—it didn't happen.

12

Having dipped her toe into some real showbiz waters made it tough for Britney to go home to Kentwood and enroll in local talent shows. She'd been there, done that, and was soooo ready to move on.

By this time, a certain TV show was soooo ready to have her.

"I love performing more than anything and having people hear my music."

On the tour bus, she and her dancers play a game called Questions. "Everybody writes a question on a piece of paper. You go around in a circle and pick one, and you have to answer—no matter what." [*Girls' Life*]

She wanted to be a star.

Working with a professional talent manager, she enrolled at the prestigious Off-Broadway Dance Center and the Professional Performing Arts School. The training was rigorous, but it was there that Britney really blossomed. Soon she was landing commercials, and, in 1991, her first stage play. Titled *Ruthless,* it was based on an old thriller called *The Bad Seed.* "At ten, I was playing this really bad child who seems real sweet, but she's evil, too," Britney detailed in her record company bio, adding, "It was so much fun!"

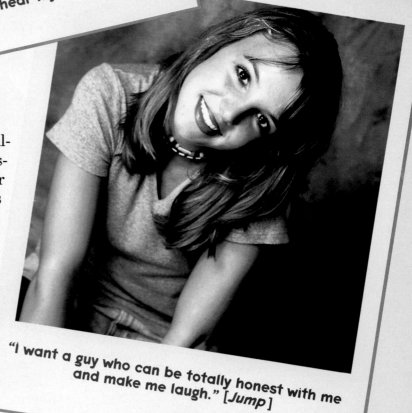

"I want a guy who can be totally honest with me and make me laugh." [*Jump*]

Britney
Spears

The Mouske-Years

"[MMC] is when I realized I had a major love of music."

Back in the early 1960s, one of the most popular kids' shows on TV was *The Mickey Mouse Club*. It featured a cast of a dozen or so talented kids performing comedy, music, dance, and acting in skits and mini-movies. It was a huge hit.

today. **Keri Russell,** who won a Golden Globe award for her starring role in TV's *Felicity,* was a Mouseketeer in the early '90s.

JC Chasez was another member of the show—he was on for most of the run. Fans know JC best today as a charter member of the band 'N Sync.

Justin Timberlake is also a *Mickey Mouse* alum, although he didn't come on board until the show's last two seasons. He is best known today for being the heartthrob of 'N Sync.

And then there was Britney. Originally turned away when she first auditioned, by the age of 11 she was back for good, hired as one of 20 talented Mouseketeers.

Because the show taped its segments in

> "Once, my headset and mic...which is connected to this [receiver] that was taped to my body...fell off. I put it back on quickly, but it was so embarrassing. Thank goodness it was during my last song. If it had been at the beginning, I would have died." [*Teen People*]

Six degrees of Britney: She went to school in McComb, Mississippi—hometown of another young singer/actress: Brandy.

Rental System CLARK

Britney's in the driver's seat—of her career, anyway!

In 1989, the Disney Channel decided to create a new version of that show—completely updated and featuring the most talented troupe of tweens and teens casting directors could find. It, too, was incredibly popular. The new show would eventually last for seven seasons, and would produce some of the hottest names in young Hollywood

[series] I ever did," she detailed in *Girls' Life.* "Back then, we were all so happy to be together and to be on the show. I don't think we focused on anything else."

Of her costars, Britney candidly remembers that "JC was totally rambunctious back then," and that Keri "was older and basically stuck with the older kids."

By the time *MMC* ended two years later, Britney had come to a decision. "That is when I realized I had a major love of music because we got to sing and dance and act on the show. And that's when I realized I loved to sing."

And that was where she decided to put her energy.

Britney bonds with singing bud, Jennifer Paige, whose song "Crush" was a hit.

Orlando, Florida, again Britney's home life had to be compromised: For the next two years, she spent half the year in Louisiana and the other half in Florida. The experience was more than worth the sacrifices: It focused her.

"*The Mickey Mouse Club* was the first

MMC

He Said, She Said...

JC & BRITNEY TELL IT LIKE IT IS!

There are two sides to every story—and we all know that two heads are better than one when it comes to solving problems. At least that's how the crew at the *Mickey Mouse Club* see it. Each month, right here in *16*, two-by-two, they'll tackle a stack of your letters and give you the male point of view and the female too! This time up at bat—18-year-old **JC Chasez** and 12-year-old **Britney Spears**.

MY FRIENDS WON'T LIKE HIM

I like this guy and I think he likes me, because he always smiles at me, but he's very shy. I'm tempted to ask him out on a date, but I'm shy, too. The other problem is my friends don't think he's cute, even though I do. I know I shouldn't care what they think, but I'm afraid they'll make fun of me. One of my friends told me he has a girlfriend, but I don't know if it's true. Please tell me what I should do.
Stephanie, Muscatine, IA

BRITNEY: "THINK FOR YOURSELF"

"First, I think you should find out if he has a girlfriend. Then, find out if he likes you. If he asks you to go out with him and you really like him, say yes. It doesn't matter what your friends say, it's what you say. Do what you think is right."

JC: "TAKE CHARGE"

"If you like this guy, and he seems to like you, I say go for it. If you're both shy, someone has to take the initiative—it might as well be you! If you don't, he may move on and you'll regret missing your chance. As for what your friends think of him—forget that! It's your choice, not theirs.

I'M IN LOVE WITH SOMEONE FAMOUS!

I have a really big problem. I like this guy who was in the movie *3 Ninjas*. His name is Michael Treanor and he played Rocky. I think he's really cute. I know I'll probably never get the chance to meet him, but I think about him all the time. If I write him a letter, he'll probably read it and say "who cares" because he doesn't know me. Help! What should I do?
Lindsay, Downers Grove, IL

BRITNEY: "WRITE RIGHT AWAY"

"If you really like Michael a lot, then you should write to him. If he doesn't write you back, it's not the end of the world. You will meet cuter and nicer boys in your life. But definitely take a chance."

JC: "ACTORS ARE PEOPLE TOO"

"Popular people are people too—they just know a couple more people! If you have a crush on him, it's okay. If you want to write to him, go for it! You never know what might happen. Give it a try and good luck!"

I CAN'T MAKE UP MY MIND

I have a big problem. I like a guy in my class named Ryan. He seems to like me, but I'm not sure. I used to go out with a guy named Chris, who is now my best friend. Chris says he wants to go out with me again, but I really like Ryan. I don't want to hurt Chris. What should I do?
Allison, Orange, CA

BRITNEY: "FIRST THIN[K]"

"First find [out]... Then figure [out]... like best. Tr[y]... the boy you[r]... want to be [with?]... you made a s[?]... the boy you l[ike]...

JC: "BE TRUE TO [YOU?]"

"If you like Ryan, t[hen the] one you should be with. I[f Chris is] your friend, he should set his personal feelings aside and try to be understanding. Just be sure to go easy on him, since you are his friend."

Back in their Mouseketeer days, circa 1994, Britney and JC contributed to an advice column in *16* magazine, called "He Said, She Said . . ."

Grace Under Fire's **JON PAUL STEUR** likes to be called JP...**JOHN STAMOS** (*Full House's* Uncle Jesse) is dating a model.

Homeward—And Homework—Bound

Britney was going on 14 when *The Mickey Mouse Club* was canceled. She returned to Kentwood, determined that singing was her future.

But she was also determined not to miss anymore of her "normal" teen years. And not to come home as some kind of diva, in spite of her TV experience. That part wasn't tough. She related in *Girls' Life*: "Coming from such a small town, everyone really knew me before, so it wasn't like anyone was putting on an act around me. My friends and I still acted stupid around each other, like always."

"i had a relationship, but it didn't work out. With me on the road, there has to be a major amount of trust." [*People*]

"One day i was jumping on my trampoline and singing and my mom realized i could carry a tune. i think that was when i first thought about going into entertainment."

Will little sister Jamie Lynn follow in Brit's boot-steps? Too early to tell, but it's clear the sisters are best buds.

Meeting the guys of 98° was extra cool— left to right, that's Nick, Jeff, Drew, and Justin making that "Britney sandwich."

She dove into school, shopping and hanging with her buds.

She chose to go to a private school called the Park Lane School, just up the highway in nearby McComb, Mississippi. Academically, her best subjects were English— she loves to write—and history. Her worst? Math. "It was too complicated, especially when I was trying to learn it. At least with history and English, you're going to use that, and history is interesting. But geometry—you're like, 'when am I going to use this in my life?' You're not. And that makes it more frustrating."

Britney's "beauty" secrets: drink lots of water, eat well, and get lots of sleep.

Of course, going back to the classroom wasn't just about reading, writing, and isosceles triangles. She enrolled there with bright hopes of freewheeling teen fun—but the year didn't turn out as she'd envisioned. She was unhappy, she has revealed, feeling that there were too many cliques, and too many stuffy rules to follow. Yet, she gamely tried to fit in. "I did the homecoming and prom thing," she told *People,* adding, "and I was totally bored."

When she opened for 'N Sync, at first the girls in the audience were disappointed—until, that is, she started to rock out!

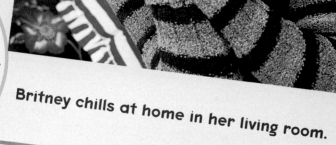

Britney chills at home in her living room.

Britney Spears

"i broke up [with my boyfriend] before any of my success happened. He became insecure with himself, i felt...i was really head over heels in love. i don't think i'll ever love somebody like that again...[but] i just woke up one day and click! it was gone."

Paying her dues included many, many visits to radio stations across the country—doing on-air interviews and talking about her album.

When Britney did her mall tour, she sang four songs and was accompanied by a pair of dancers.

good enough to submit to a pro.

She was right.

Her mom sent it—on a tip—to a prominent New York City entertainment attorney. He was immediately blown away. He signed on as Britney's co-manager and soon snared her a real audition at Jive Records, home to the Backstreet Boys.

Britney had no musical accompaniment when she auditioned: Her voice was her instrument. That's all it took. On the strength of her *a cappella* performance in front of Jive Records execs, she was signed to a contract immediately. An entire program was developed around her, so everyone would soon know her name, her sound, her face.

It was 1998, and the reign of Britney Spears had officially begun!

Britney has music on the CD-ROM of the Backstreet Boys All Access Home video pack.

In March 1999, she had arthroscopic surgery on her left knee to excise cartilage damaged while rehearsing for the *Sometimes* video. Five weeks of rest were prescribed.

Uh-huh. According to her Jive Records bio, that year at school "was fun for a while—but I started getting really itchy to get out again and see the world."

Clearly, Britney's showbiz dreams were never far off. She continued to study dance, and even taught herself moves by hanging out in her room for hours, studying Michael Jackson videos. She also recorded music and made demo [showbiz speak for demonstration] tapes. When she was 15, she'd made a tape she believed was

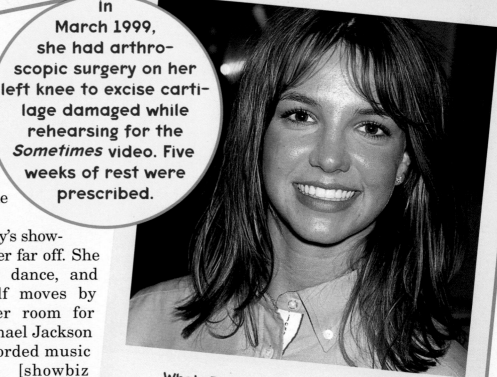

Who's Britney's fantasy dinner date? Brad Pitt's high on the list!

A Fast 'N' Furious Fact File

Basic Britney

Real Full Name: Britney Jean Spears

Birthday: December 2, 1981

Astro Sign: Sagittarius

Parents: Britney's dad is Jamie, he's a construction contractor by trade. Her mom is Lynne, a second-grade teacher.

Brother: Bryan is 21. Of him, Britney has said, "He's a good brother. He is sometimes the father type, always looking out for me. Sometimes, he drives me crazy!"

Sister: Jamie Lynn is eight.

Hair Color: Light brown with blond streaks

Eye Color: Brown

Height: 5′ 4″

School: Britney's enrolled in the University of Nebraska home school program. She's set to graduate high school in the spring of 2000.

Faves & Raves

Colors: Baby blue; anything bright and vibrant

Stylin': Tommy jeans, tank tops, twin sets

Mall Stores: Abercrombie & Fitch, Armani Exchange, Tommy Hilfiger

Of opening for 'N Sync, she admitted, "It hasn't always been easy . . . since there are all girls in the audience. But I ultimately am able to win them over."

Jewelry: Britney's big on her diamond stud earrings
Music: Mariah Carey, Whitney Houston
Movies: "Chick flicks" like *Titanic, Stepmom, Steel Magnolias*
TV Shows: She doesn't watch much—only *Dawson's Creek* occasionally and sometimes *Felicity,* because her old bud Keri is "so breathtaking, so cute."
Sport: Basketball, gymnastics
Food: Blackened shrimp, mashed potatoes, onion rings, chips dipped in hot cheese sauce, her mom's grilled cheese sandwiches. "I eat what I want to eat, I just don't overdo anything," Britney explains.

"If there's one thing I'm great at, it's shopping. Let's just say I know my way around a mall."
[*Jump*]

A football jersey's just for posing: her main sport is gymnastics.

Britney
Spears

Posing with singer Marsha Milan.

Home Is Where The Heart Is

She Lives: In Kentwood, Louisiana, population 2,600. An hour's drive north-west of New Orleans, it actually sits on the Mississippi border.

Her House: Is a ranch-style, meaning everything's on one level. The living room is wood-paneled, and on those walls are mementos of Britney's career—including a 1992 appearance on TV's *Star Search*. The shelves are laden with her brother's sports trophies.

Her Room: "It's a girly-room," she admits. "It's got baby blue carpet, a white bean bag chair." Floral patterns are every-where, lots of frills, throw cushions, and dolls—lots of dolls.

Secret: She loves airplane food!

Fast Food Snack: Anything at Jack in the Box

Ice Cream Flavor: Ben & Jerry's Cookie Dough; Pralines & Cream

Brit Lit: Romance novels; *The Horse Whisperer* is the last book she read.

Magazine: *Cosmopolitan*

Word That's Not A Word: Stomper. "My mama says that all the time," she exclaimed in *Entertainment Weekly*, "like, I had a good day, but you put a stomper on me."

Songs On Her Album: Britney's personal favorites are "…Baby One More Time" and "From the Bottom of My Broken Heart."

Crush Boy: Ben Affleck, because "he's so cute—and he doesn't have a girl-friend now, does he?"

Being on the road is hard, but Britney tries to get home "about every six weeks so I get to see my family and friends and do completely normal stuff."

"I collect dolls, so dolls are everywhere—porcelain, collectible dolls, and *Little Women* dolls. I also have angels everywhere. I collect them—and pictures galore. It's a small room, but cute."

Her 'Tude: At home, Britney is careful to be cool but not chilly. "If I come out being Miss Prima Donna, that wouldn't be smart."

What's On Her Answering Machine: Random bits of songs she's writing.

What's A Hit With BRIT

🙂 Being recognized by fans: as long as the encounter doesn't get too intense. She told a reporter, "Fans are just, like, crazy. It's flattering, but sometimes they get a little overbearing and you're like, 'Stay back!'"

The best part of being Britney? Getting to travel and meet talented people.

"I would describe myself as honest, trustworthy, and just a sweet girl that anyone can talk to." [*Girls' Life*]

😊 Shopping: anytime, any mall, any city in any country.

😊 Talking on the phone, hanging with friends.

What's The Pits With Brit

☹ Driving—she admits she's not great at it.

☹ Zits—yep, she still gets 'em.

☹ That "preview" of the Backstreet Boys' *Millennium* album that got tacked onto the end of her CD. "If I would've known I had a choice, I wouldn't have done it," she candidly said in an interview.

☹ TV's outrageous *South Park,* which she has called sacrilegious.

☹ TV's *Felicity*—although Keri is her friend, the show is a little too neurotic for her!

Britney and designer Tommy Hilfiger goofed around for the cameras.

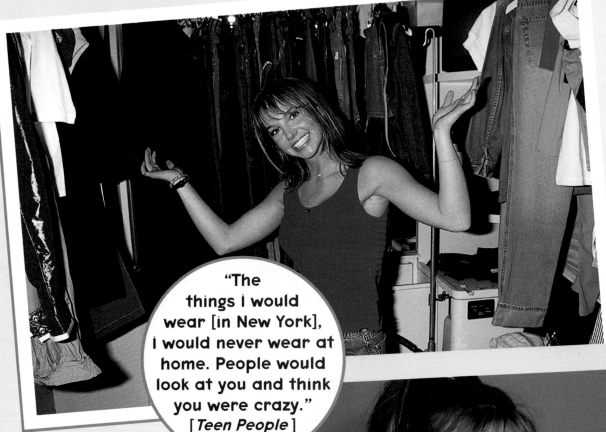

"The things i would wear [in New York], i would never wear at home. People would look at you and think you were crazy."
[*Teen People*]

A Quick 'N' Cool Q & A
Britney dishes about 'N Sync, the Backstreet Boys—and boys she goes for.

Q: Of all the places you've toured, which is your favorite?
A: The most interesting was probably Singapore, because it was so beautiful—but really, really hot. And the shopping was great, since all the people there are so small—everything fit me!

Q: What do you miss most when you're on the road?
A: My family. But I'm on the phone with my mom all the time. We're so close, so when I come home we really bond.

Q: Do you have a boyfriend?
A: No, I don't.

Britney's favorite teacher was the one she had in third grade, "Miss Hughes—she was awesome!"

Q: What kind of boys do you usually go for?

A: I like someone with a lot of confidence, someone who's happy with himself. The relationship has to be about trust. A guy who's really possessive and unsure of himself—no trust—that doesn't attract me at all.

Q: Were you starstruck the first time you met the Backstreet Boys?

A: I wasn't really starstruck with any of them except Kevin. He was so beautiful—he's prettier in person than in pictures. And I was like, "Oh, my goodness," I didn't know what to say.

Q: So what did you say?

A: Well, he said, "Haven't I met you before? I met you in Atlanta." And I was like, "Oh, really?" But I knew I'd

Britney told *Teen Celebrity* magazine that two perfect songs to dance to at your prom would be "Brown-Eyed Girl" and "Wonderful Tonight."

For fun with her buds, Britney's into going for rides to the beach.

never been to Atlanta. Still, I acted as if I had been there, like a real stupid-head.

Q: You toured with 'N Sync— what was that like?

A: They're like big brothers to me, they're all so goofy and fun. I probably know JC and Justin the best, since we did *The Mickey Mouse Club* together.

Q: Most embarrassing onstage moment?

A: That's easy. B*Witched was onstage before me, and for some reason, there was a cupcake up there that I didn't see until it was too late. And I had on these major platform shoes—all of a sudden, I slipped and fell. I was so embarrassed, there was an arena full of people looking at me, on my butt.

SCOOP

A rare shot of Britney wearing glasses.

Crimped hair is for special occasions— like the American Music Awards.

Britney Spears

Britney's advice for would-be singers: "The job isn't all the glamour that you see on TV. You have to love what you are doing, and you have to love to sing. If so, then go for it." [*Girls' Life*]

Britney was surprised when "...Baby One More Time" debuted on the top of the charts. "When they told me it was number one, I went, like, 'Whaaat?'"

Britney Spears: Superstar!

"I want to be an artist that everyone can relate to, who's young and happy and fun."

That was the vision. It was true to the music and to who she is, as an artist and as a person. As she explained to *Rolling Stone* magazine, "It made sense to go pop, because I can dance to it, it's more me." Yep. Britney is young, fresh, upbeat, optimistic, and wholesome. She performs pop music, pure and simple, bouncy and funky. Most important, she sings about things people her age can relate to: crushing and being crushed by love, wanting to belong, being so curious about life!

When Brit needs a pig-out pick-me-up, she heads for the freezer where a pint of Ben & Jerry's chocolate chip cookie dough ice cream usually awaits!

Being constantly photographed comes naturally to her now.

"i'm all about trees and grass," she admits.

Lucky for Britney, she was in the right place at the right time—with, finally, the right team behind her. A multi-pronged plan was devised, and all through 1998 she worked to launch the dream she'd held in her heart since her earliest memories.

...Baby One More Time :
The Album

That same year, she recorded her first album for which she composed the track, "Sometimes." Each line of all of the other songs, however, was also approved by her. And even though they were written by professionals, Britney did suggest a change or two. The original lyrics to "Born to Make You Happy" weren't really happening for her. "This may be a little old

A definite "perk" of being the hottest girl singer around is hanging with sizzling boy bands like 98°.

Britney did the red-carpet arrival thing at the American Music Awards.

When she feels the need to burn some extra calories, she pops in her fave hip-hop CD and works out for at least 20 minutes.

Hundreds of thousands of fans first became aware of her in cyberspace. Within just a few months, her Website got more hits than the previous reigning Internet champ—Jenny McCarthy.

for me," she told her producers. "I don't want to go over the top." Presto—some of the lyrics were rewritten. The album was released on January 12, 1999.

Britney Spears: The Web site, E-mail Address, And 800 Number

Maybe that's a strange way to kick off a musical career—then again, maybe not.

Britney Spears: The Mall Tour

After signing the contract and laying down the tracks for her album, she embarked on a singing tour of shopping malls around the country—going to where her natural audience hung out. "It was crazy," she said in *People*. "No one knew who I was, but I could see they really enjoyed the music. And, I got a lot of shopping done!"

But it was also grueling. In one

Britney Spears

Britney once admitted that if she could be any superhero, she'd pick the Pink Power Ranger!

Tommy Hilfiger photo session, when she got a call from the president of Jive Records. "They asked me if I was sitting down," she told a reporter, "because what they were about to say might make me faint." Not only had the single debuted at number one, so had the CD. "I'd hoped and dreamed, but I never honestly expected to have a number-one album."

Did she celebrate? He*llo*? She stayed up all night with her friends, kickin' it to the wee hours.

stretch, she actually toured 37 cities in 21 days. Of course, it wasn't all singing and shopping: She also visited radio stations and did countless on-air interviews.

"...Baby One More Time": The Single

Britney will never forget the first time she heard her single on the radio. "I had just gotten off a plane, and I was in the car, ready to go home—and it came on the radio. And it was major! It was like we'd accomplished so much!"

Britney Spears In History

January 19, 1999, is a day Britney Spears won't ever forget. She was in West Palm Beach, Florida, getting ready for the

Between scenes on her "... Baby One More Time" video, Britney played cards and board games with her dancers.

"This is not right. If you want me to reach four-year-olds, then OK." The best way to reach her own peer group, Britney thought, was to set the scene in a place teenagers can relate to—like high school. Tidbit: The video was shot at the same school where the movie *Grease* lensed.

Her wardrobe was also a Britney brainstorm—specifically the shirt being tied, and the knee-highs—"so it wouldn't be boring or cheesy," she explained.

"Sometimes": The Second Single

Released on March 20, 1999, it hit the charts running, vaulting up to number one in only a few weeks. *Billboard* called it: "Pure up-tempo pop at its most uplifting." Fans agreed.

Britney In Concert

Although she's headliner-friendly for sure, much of Britney's concertizing has been as an 'N Sync opener. And yeah, it was kind of scary since she knew all the girls in the audience were really there for Justin, JC, Lance, Joey, and Chris. She revealed to *Entertainment Weekly*, "I was so nervous because it was already out that a girl was opening up for 'N Sync. I'd walk out there for my first two [songs], they were like 'Boo!' [But then] they'd go crazy."

...Baby One More Time: The Video

Maybe she didn't write the lyrics, but when it came to acting them out on video, Britney had lots of input. Output, too—she totally booted the original concept that was presented to her. In a *Rolling Stone* interview, she revealed the video that would have been: "It was this really bizarre video idea, this animated Power Ranger-y thing. I said,

A Model Teen

In spite of the high-gloss Hilfiger layouts and the just nikki :) cover, Britney considers herself *no way* a model—nor would she

explained in her record company bio. "I need to sing, and I love to travel."

A Role Model Teen

She didn't ask to be a role model, but *whomp*, there it is: It comes with the territory. And that's cool with Britney, who expressed her feelings in *Rolling Stone*: "You want to be a good example for kids out there, and not do something stupid. [Some] kids have low self-esteem, and then the peer pressure comes and they [might] go into a wrong crowd. That's when the bad stuff starts happening, drugs and stuff. I think if they find something that keeps them happy, writing, drawing, anything like that—then they'll have confidence."

Britney thinks Jennifer Love Hewitt is one of the best-dressed stars around.

want to be. "I'm not a model. [Doing that] was a lot of fun, [but] I don't know how models just sit and smile. I got to ice skate and goof around, and in the case of just nikki :) to keep the clothes, too," she related to a reporter.

A Normal Teen

"I go home every six weeks, so I get to see my family and friends and do completely normal stuff—girl stuff, like we'll go to a mall and hang out," Britney told *USA Today*. Sure, she gets homesick sometimes, but not for a second would she give up her career. "I've done the prom thing, but it's only once a year," she

Britney's been on lots of talk shows, including The Ricki Lake Show and Donny and Marie.

Britney Spears

Even though Britney's from Louisiana, she's a real New York Yankees fan.

your video on MTV—this is unreal." [*People*]

Did You Know?

That's really her doing the backflip in the ...*Baby One More Time* video: all those years of gymnastics paid off!

Any way you slice it—take the record charts, MTV video countdown, concert grosses, TV appearances, or modeling gigs—Britney Spears, circa 1999, is a superstar. And, judging by her attitude, one happy little superstar. "If I wasn't in love with my job and in love with music, I would be homesick and going crazy."

How Cool Is That?

"It's so awesome just to hear your song on the radio and see

Her favorite places: Florida [to chill out], and New York City—"i don't know what i'd do without the energy i get from being there," she said in *Teen Celebrity* magazine.

Britney Discography

CD
Britney Spears,
...Baby One More Time

Tracks
- "...Baby One More Time"
[single, released 1/99]
- "You Drive Me Crazy"
- "Sometimes" [single, released 3/99]
- "Soda Pop"
- "Born to Make You Happy"
- "From the Bottom of My Broken Heart"
- "I Will Be There"
- "I Will Still Love You"
[duet with Don Philip]
- "Thinkin' About You"
- "E-Mail My Heart"
- "The Beat Goes On"

Britney was profiled on *Teen People's* TV special as one of the 21 Hottest Stars Under 21.

Though she's not a real cyber-freak herself, she happily connected with her fans on an AOL chat in March 1999.

SWAK: Reaching Britney

Snail Mail
Britney Spears Fan Club
P.O. Box 7022
Red Bank, NJ 07701-7022

Britney Spears
Jive Records
137-139 West 25th Street
New York, NY 10001

On the Web
www.peeps.com/britney
E-mail
britney@peeps.com

In only 11 weeks in release, Britney's album, lodged at number one more than half that time, has already sold more than two million copies.

Future Brit

"I want to be big all around the world."

What she's accomplished already is amazing: what she's aiming for is unreal. Check out her millennium plans.

More Music

Album Number Two is already being worked on. Though there's no title just yet, there is this: Britney aims to compose more of the tracks. She's writing them now.

A Dream Duet: "I would love to do a duet with Madonna," she said, "because she's just like, really out there and I think it would be a shocker to people."

More Acting

Dawson's Creek nabbed her for three episodes. When the deal was being done, Britney declared, "I won't play somebody mean, and I won't play myself."

A Show Of Her Own—as you're reading this, writers are furiously working on a series for Britney that would showcase her acting, singing, and dancing skills. Could be a comedy, or possibly even a drama.

What it won't be is ready before March, 2000 and what it won't do is take time away from her music. That comes first.

A Movie Star? If she has her way, oh, yeah. But the role would have to be just right, the story itself something she likes.

More Education

Although she will have graduated high school well into her career, Britney would like to attend college one day.